BOSNIA

Ο ΦΙΛΕΛΕ...

ΗΜΕΡΗΣΙΑ ΕΦΗΜΕΡΙΣ...

ΖΗΤΑ ΠΕΙΘΑ...

...immunity
ments that do not
plications for

...six public interest
immunity certificates
during his year at the
Home Office on security
grounds.

INTERNATIONAL

erald Tribu...

PUBLISHED WITH THE NEW YORK TIMES AND THE WASHINGTON POST

London, Tuesday, March 8, 1994

Clint...
Is N...
Des...

Α ΚΑΙ ΘΑ ΣΥΓΚΑΛΕΣΕΙ

ΩΝ ΠΥ...
ΕΥΡΩ...

'Cleansers' of Muslims Show No Sign of Yielding

By Roger Cohen
New York Times Service

ZVORNIK, Bosnia-Herzegovina — Up through a ghostly terrain of smashed and ransacked former Muslim homes, Branko Grujic led the way, intent on showing off his crowning contribution to what he calls the victory of Serbian Orthodox Christianity over Islam in Bosnia.

Mr. Grujic, the mayor of this northeastern Bosnian town now controlled by Serbs and completely "cleansed" of its 40,000 prewar Muslim inhabitants, has a pet project. It stands atop the escarpment that overlooks Zvornik and the meandering sweep of the Drina River.

Arriving at the summit of the cliff, Mr. Grujic paused to kiss a wooden cross he has had erected before declaring: "The Turks destroyed the Serbian church that was here when they arrived in Zvornik in 1463. Now we are rebuilding the church and reclaiming this as Serbian land forever and t..."

There is indeed a cruel finality to

of thousands of Muslims have been pushed out by force, many of them to Bosnian government-controlled territory around Srebrenica and Tuzla.

Such activity, and the uncompromising attitude of Mr. Grujic, suggest that Serbian readiness to accept new peace proposals from the United States may be scant.

Serbs in general remain committed to holding onto land they have seized by force and

---

The UN deploys troops around T...
in preparation for an aid

appear to have little...
Bosnian politic...
with Mus...
"Look
point...
shif...

Γράφει: Α. Λυκαύγης

Τ ΙΣ σοβαρές του ανησυχίες,
εξελίξεις κι ενδεχόμενα α
ρό...τος της Δημοκρατίας Γλα
...ιβούλιο την κατ...
..νέσθαι,

EL

EL

Le gouvernement israélien divisé face aux colons extrémistes

...tractations continuent en Israël à pro-
...rée au gouvernement du parti
...Tsomet du général Rafaël
...auche Meretz —
...ouhaitée par M. Rabin,
...Shass, qui

opposé les membres du gouvernem...
mesures à prendre contre les...
veille, entre 25 000 et 30...
dont quelques milliers...
à Tel-Aviv pour réc...
diate des extrém...
occupés, voire...
des colons.

PIDEN «DEMOCRACIA PARIT...

stras europe...

1 PRECIO: 100 PTS.

BOMB FEAR
53 DIE IN

Le Monde
75501 Paris Cedex 15

FONDATEUR : HUBERT BEUV

«...sutución». ... réndum será una prueba más de ... Moldavia ha elegido un ... la democracia, don-... nos son

ΛΙΤΙΚΗ ΗΓΕΣΙΑ

ΩΝ

ΤΗΣ

...is no cr...
to be a very different thing ...
...t suggested that the Republi-
...airly attacking him and added:
...n people will be outraged if any-
...s as an excuse for not doing the

R

DAILY MIRROR, Tuesday, March 8, 1994

CSA PAY BUNGLE
LEFT ME BRO

ηγοί κομμάτων
κληρίδη εκτάκτω

...οδήλως αρνητικές για την Κύ
...ο της Ευρώπης, συμμερίζεται
..., που: Σύντομα θα θέσει μπροσ
...ειμένου να δρομολογηθούν απ
...αποτροπή χωριστός εκπροσώπ
...σης των Τ/Κυπρίων.

...Κι αυτό προκύπτει απο χθε
...νη συνάντηση του Προεδρο.
...με τον προεδρο της Βουλή
...λλεξη Γαλανό, που τον ενημι
...νω σε καποιες λεπτομε-
...προαγονται στς
...ο το

A DIVORCED father has wrongly had £634 a month docked from his pay by the Child Support Agency.

The outrageous bungle has forced crane driver Roy Sullivan to:

PUT his £40,000 house up for sale.

SELL his Ford Escort ...r, and

HAVE his phone cut off. Desperate 36-year-old ...is now off work ...g from a stomach ...stress.

...the CSA ...puter for

agency fixed Roy's main-tenance deductions at £1,004 a month.

Then it found he was being charged not only for his two daughters - but for a child who isn't his.

The agency apologised and reduced the deduction order attached to his earnings.

But Roy, from Cardiff, still hasn't had a refund. He said: "I earn £300 a week but after deductions I didn't have enough left to pay my £300 mortgage.

"I've had the 'For Sale' ...gn up for several weeks. ...rests of justice over. ...the PIIC does not ...view."
...as stated ...as W ...Matr... ...haf ...Scot

My bank manager can't see any option as I haven't any money left to live on.

"I appealed against the CSA assessment ... summer but they ... no notice. The ... forced my emp... hand it all over ... "I can't bel... dictatorial ... agency behav...

App...

Labour Jones, w... Roy's appalli... Th... bank... big... n...

MUNDO
DEL SIGLO VEINTIUNO

...réis jamás; y si desesperáis seguid trabajando. (Burke)

...IA INTERNACIO...

Published by Raintree Steck-Vaughn Publishers, an imprint of Steck-Vaughn Company

Designed and produced by Aladdin Books
Editor: Jen Green
Designer: Tessa Barwick
Consultant: Catherine Bradley

Raintree Steck-Vaughn Publishers staff
Project Manager: Julie Klaus
Editor: Kathy DeVico
Electronic Production: Scott Melcer

Library of Congress Cataloging-in-Publication Data
Flint, David, 1946-
     Bosnia; can there ever be peace? / David Flint.
        p.   cm. — (Topics in the news)
     "Special edition."
     Includes index.
     ISBN 0-8172-4176-0
     1. Yugoslav War, 1991- — Bosnia and Herzegovina — Juvenile literature.   2. Bosnia and Herzegovina — History — 1992- — Juvenile literature.   [1. Bosnia and Herzegovina — History — 1992-   2. Yugoslav War, 1991-]   I. Title.
II. Series.
DR1313.3.F56   1996
949.7'42024—dc20   95-11749
                                                                                      CIP
                                                                                      AC

Printed and bound in Belgium
1 2 3 4 5 6 7 8 9 0   99 98 97 96 95

Special Edition

BOSNIA

Can There Ever Be Peace?

David Flint

Thousands of civilians have lost their lives during the conflict in Bosnia.

RSVP

**RAINTREE
STECK-VAUGHN**
P U B L I S H E R S
The Steck-Vaughn Company

Austin, Texas

A soldier fires a bazooka during a skirmish between warring sides in Bosnia.

War in Bosnia

The conflict has been one of the bloodiest in recent history.

After nearly three years of war, there is a tentative cease-fire in Bosnia. A truce was called among the main warring factions in December, 1994. However, there is still a long way to go before true peace can be attained.

Bosnia used to be part of a larger country called Yugoslavia. In 1991 some of the republics that made up Yugoslavia split off and declared independence. These included Slovenia, Croatia, Bosnia, and Macedonia. Serbia and its ally, Montenegro, were all that was left of Yugoslavia.

The former Yugoslavia

Yugoslav Republics Battle for Land

On the breakup of Yugoslavia, the peoples of the region became involved in a war over territory. Fighting broke out first in Slovenia and then in Croatia. In 1992 the conflict flared up in Bosnia.

There has been enormous media coverage of the Bosnian war in Western countries. News features have highlighted the major issues of the war, such as refugees and the cities under siege. Less well understood, however, are the roots of the conflict, which go back many generations. The latest news reports concentrate on daily life in this shattered country and current hopes for a peaceful and final end to the conflict.

🔥 *Areas of fighting in Bosnia, Slovenia, and Croatia*

⬤ *Areas declared "safe havens" by the United Nations*

A Serb soldier looks out over the besieged city of Gorazde in 1994.

Cities Under Siege

Civilians don't have enough food or water.

Since the fighting began in Bosnia, hundreds of thousands of innocent civilians have been caught up in the conflict. The most recent and continuing siege is that in Bihac, which had been declared a UN "safe haven" in 1992.

In August 1994, thousands of people fled into Croatia, as the Bosnian government forces started to crush a year-long revolt by rebel Muslims in the Bihac region. They were soon counterattacked by Serb troops, who gained ground in the region in November. Meanwhile, civilians who remain in Bihac, or in other cities that are under siege, are left with very little food to eat or water to drink. Their lives are in constant danger.

Who's Fighting Who?

The grim situation in Bihac has also increased the pressure that was already on the international community to take a stand and intervene. In October 1994, President Bill Clinton threatened to send U. S. troops to Bosnia. But this threat only led to a breakdown of trust between Europe and the United States. On November 28, the Western powers recognized that Bihac was lost to the Bosnian Serbs and proposed a plan for demilitarization in exchange. In addition, Great Britain, Russia, and France prepared to offer the Bosnian Serbs a form of alliance with Serbia, provided that Serbia put pressure on the Bosnian Serbs to stop the fighting.

In the besieged cities, civilians wait in line for hours for bread.

UN Convoys Bring Food to Besieged Cities

Food and medicine had almost run out in cities besieged by Serbs, such as Sarajevo and Srebrenica, by winter 1992. The United Nations (UN) became involved in airlifting relief supplies into Bosnia. However, the fighting prevented convoys that were carrying the crucial supplies from reaching the cities. The UN sent in troops on a humanitarian mission to guarantee the delivery of aid. Despite these measures, aid convoys are still being prevented from getting through.

A UN convoy reaches Srebrenica in 1993.

Hungry civilians rush to a supply convoy.

UN Relief Convoys Blocked

In September, General Ratko Mladic, the Bosnian Serb military commander, returned, making threats against the NATO/UN forces. His army blocked all UN military and humanitarian convoys that were traveling through Serb-held areas and closed Sarajevo airport, cutting off an already small food supply. Despite the cease-fire, the UN has failed to persuade the Bosnian Serbs to allow the reopening of the roads that go in and out of Sarajevo.

Thousands flee the fighting

Refugee Crisis in Bosnia

Muslim refugees seek safety in the city of Tuzla.

What Is Ethnic Cleansing?

Western countries have been shocked by reports of "ethnic cleansing" in Bosnia. Serb soldiers conquering territory have intimidated Muslims and Croats and driven them from their homes. In some cases, Serbs have deliberately killed leaders of the local communities. The inhabitants have fled, leaving ghost villages behind. The international community has condemned the Serbs, but in 1993 both Muslims and Croats used similar tactics.

Refugees wait and hope in a gymnasium.

The fighting in Yugoslavia has forced over three million people to leave their homes, the most in Europe since World War II. Many refugees are forced to leave at a minute's notice, only able to take with them what they can carry. Many flee to the cities; others go to neighboring countries.

On the move, the refugees face many difficulties and dangers. Many must walk long distances in poor weather conditions, with little protection from rain, etc. Women and children suffer the most, worn down by fear and hunger. Some refugees reach "safety," only to find themselves trapped in besieged cities without the resources to feed them or the facilities to house them. In some cases, the local population has been swamped by the massive number of refugees, and families must sleep in schools or even gymnasiums (right).

The Detention Camps

The detention camps are another aspect of ethnic cleansing. Refugees report that the Serbs have rounded up Muslim and Croat civilians and captured soldiers, and have either killed them or held them in camps in northern Bosnia. The prisoners are crowded together, often in unsanitary conditions, and not given enough food. The United Nations estimates that 9,300 have been imprisoned and thousands killed, a fraction of the 150,000 thought to have died in the fighting so far.

A detention camp run by Serbs at Manjaca in northeast Bosnia

Refugees Face an Uncertain Future

Some 2,800,000 people are thought to be displaced within Bosnia. Over 500,000 refugees from the former Yugoslavia are in Croatia, 400,000 in Serbia, 400,000 in Germany, and another 350,000 in other European countries.

Attempts by the UN to evacuate refugees from besieged towns, such as Gorazde and Tuzla, often fail. Sometimes UN negotiations with Serb militias do not ensure the refugees' safe passage. The Muslim-led Bosnian government also argues against the evacuation of civilians, saying that it plays into the hands of the Serb or Croat forces who are trying to capture territory. Once the people flee, the soldiers can overrun the city and then move on to their next target.

UN troops arrive by air for a difficult tour of duty.

Can the UN Police the Cease-Fire?

Throughout the conflict in Bosnia, the UN has tried to negotiate a settlement among the warring parties. In September 1992, Yugoslavia (Serbia and Montenegro) was expelled from the UN. In July 1992, the UN began its rescue mission to airlift supplies into Sarajevo. It declared certain cities "safe havens" but did not have the troops to make the havens secure. It then took on several tasks: to protect the aid convoys, to monitor the fighting, and also to investigate war crimes.

More recently, however, there have been great tensions among the peacekeeping allies. The UN was under increasing pressure to use NATO air power against the Serbs but was reluctant to appear biased. Despite this reluctance, in November 1994, NATO combat aircraft were called in to warn off the Bosnian Serbs and government forces after there were serious breaches of the Sarajevo cease-fire by both sides. NATO hoped that this act might also prevent further attacks on Bihac. Also in November, President Clinton, under pressure from Congress, abandoned the Bosnian arms blockade that had been imposed by the UN—U. S. warships would no longer enforce the embargo against the Muslims. This act increased the tensions between the United States and Europe—especially Great Britain and France, who have many troops in Bosnia that could be put in danger if the Serbs retaliated. A breakdown of trust between the United States and Europe followed; Russia even threatened to break with the alliance completely. The situation in Bihac only added to the pressure on President Clinton to help the Bosnians.

UN tanks on patrol

"Not one of 50 generations on our territory has been spared the devastation of war and heavy losses."

Roots of Conflict

Like many European countries, Bosnia has a violent past.

Conflict is not new to the peoples of Bosnia. The crisis in the 1990s stems from rivalries and loyalties that are centuries old. Differences in religion and of historical circumstances combine to create a region where war has been all too common.

People of all religions have suffered in the fighting.

In A.D. 100 the Balkans were part of the Roman Empire. The Romans introduced Christianity and constructed beautiful buildings (above). Later the empire split into two halves with separate Christian traditions. Bosnia, Slovenia, and Croatia, ruled by the Western Empire, were Roman Catholic. Serbia, part of the Byzantine Empire, followed the Orthodox faith. This helps to explain differences today between Serbs, Croats, and Slovenes.

The Early History

From 1328 to 1878, Bosnia was occupied by the Turks. Many Bosnians converted to Islam, the Turkish religion, and became Muslims. Mosques were built.

Prince Lazar (below) led the Serbian forces against the Turks at the Battle of Kosovo in southern Serbia. After Serbia's defeat, the Turks dominated most of the region that became Yugoslavia.

Yugoslavia means "land of the south Slavs." During the fifth century, Slav peoples from central Europe arrived to occupy the region. But in the centuries that followed, the Slav races — Serbs, Croats, Slovenes, and others — would be dominated by foreign powers.

In the 12th century, the areas that are now Croatia and Slovenia were dominated by their neighbors, Hungary and Austria, later united as the Hapsburg Empire.

Parts of the region remained under Austro-Hungarian control until the 20th century. Because of these links, most Slavs in Slovenia and Croatia are Roman Catholic.

The Battle of Kosovo (1389) was crucial to the Turkish expansion.

In 1566 the Turks won an important victory over Hungary.

Franz I (1708–1768) was a member of the powerful Hapsburg family who ruled Austria and Hungary. The Hapsburgs controlled an empire that dominated central Europe from 1448 to 1806.

The 600th anniversary of the Battle of Kosovo was in 1989. The battle had become a symbol of Serb national pride, and the anniversary was the occasion of a display of Serbian power in the province.

To the east, Serbia enjoyed an early taste of independence. During the 9th century, it resisted the rule of the Byzantine Empire and became a powerful kingdom. In the 14th century, under Stefan Dusan (1331–1355), Serbia looked ready to expand. Its people continued to follow the Orthodox religion of the Byzantine Empire.

Bosnia was the last of the southern Slav states to achieve an independent identity. It first appeared as a separate state under Prince Kulin in the 12th century. In the 14th century, it began to expand, taking over Herzegovina to the south. Under Stephen Tvrtko (1353–1391) Bosnia grew powerful enough to rival Serbia.

However, the ambitions of the southern Slav states were crushed by a group of Turkish Muslims, called the Ottomans, who were expanding their territories across the Balkans. In 1389 Serbia was defeated by the Turks at the Battle of Kosovo. Bosnia was occupied by Turkish armies in 1328. By the 15th century, the Turks ruled most of the region. Turkish rule was harsh and often corrupt, and there were periodic attempts to rebel against them.

The Turkish advance was halted in the 17th century at the boundary, which today forms Croatia's eastern border. For the next three centuries, Austria-Hungary and the Slavs chipped away at the territory that the Turks had won.

War and Rebellion

Ban Jelacic was the native governor of Croatia in 1848. He led a Slav uprising against Hapsburg rule.

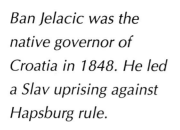

In 1815 Milos Obrenovic led a Serb revolt against the Hapsburgs. This was inspiring to Bosnians, who were under Turkish rule.

The period 1800–1918 was a time of unrest for the countries of the Balkan region. The upheaval greatly affected Bosnia and the lands around it, especially Serbia, Croatia, and Slovenia. In 1800 the northern part of Serbia was under Hapsburg control, and the south was ruled by the Turks.

In the early 1800s, there was a series of uprisings in Serbia against both Turkish and Hapsburg control. In 1815 Milos Obrenovic led the Serbs against the Hapsburgs and established a small independent Serbia with the support of Russia. Throughout the 19th century, Serbia grew in strength through its alliance with Russia. By 1882, it was recognized as a kingdom, eager to expand and challenge Hapsburg dominance.

In 1799 Croatia and Slovenia were conquered by Napoleon Bonaparte. By 1800, they had formed the eastern border of the Napoleonic Empire. But when Napoleon was defeated at the Battle of Waterloo in 1815, Hapsburg rule was reestablished. In 1848 Ban (Chief) Jelacic led the first of a series of revolts against Hapsburg rule. As a result, by 1867, Croatia had gained a certain amount of independence.

Skirmish between Slavs and Turks in 1901

In 1800 Bosnia was still ruled by the declining Turkish Empire, but in 1878 it was taken over by Austria-Hungary. Most Bosnians resented their continued domination by foreign powers and wanted instead to unite with the newly independent Serbia. Serbia had become the focus of Slav hopes for independence, and for the formation of a single state uniting all the southern Slav peoples.

By 1900, the Bosnian people, including Muslims, Orthodox Serbs, and Catholic Croats, were united in resenting foreign rule. This sparked the June 1914 assassination of Archduke Franz Ferdinand, heir to the Austro-Hungarian Empire. He was killed while in Bosnia.

Gavrilo Princip, a Bosnian Serb, was a student revolutionary. In June 1914, he shot Archduke Franz Ferdinand on a state visit to Bosnia. This incident was to push Europe into a war like no one had seen before.

More than ten million soldiers were killed during World War I. The defeat of Germany and Austria-Hungary paved the way for the formation of Yugoslavia.

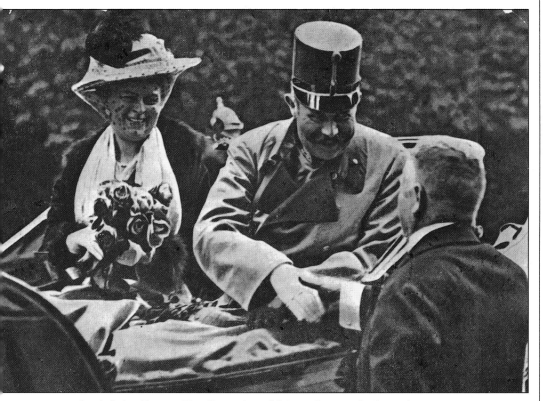

Archduke Franz Ferdinand and his wife, just before the assassination

Austria-Hungary accused Serbia of being involved in the assassination and threatened to invade. Serbia denied involvement and called on its ally, Russia, and later France and Great Britain for support. Austria-Hungary appealed to Germany and declared war on Serbia and its allies. This is how World War I began.

Throughout World War I, the movement for southern Slav unity and independence grew, especially in Serbia and Bosnia. When the war ended in a defeat for Germany and Austria-Hungary, this movement was supported by Great Britain, France, and Russia. In December 1918, the first united Yugoslavia, called "the Kingdom of the Serbs, Croats, and Slovenes" was proclaimed.

The Birth of Yugoslavia

Peter II was young when his father, King Alexander, was killed, but he took the throne in 1941. A month later, Germany invaded, and Peter fled.

In 1918 the young Kingdom of the Serbs, Croats, and Slovenes faced many problems. Most of these were a result of the rivalry between the Serbs and Croats, which had its roots in the foreign occupations of the previous centuries.

Many Serbs wanted a centralized system, which would have given them power over the whole nation. Croats and Slovenes wanted a federal system where regional governments had more control.

These disagreements made an effective government impossible. In 1929, the king, Alexander, dissolved the parliament and proclaimed his personal rule over a country he renamed Yugoslavia.

Adolf Hitler came to power in Germany in 1933, as leader of the Nazi party. His aim was to regain the territory Germany had lost after World War I and to expand eastward.

German tanks advance during World War I.

Alexander tried to break the Serbian hold on power and encourage loyalty to the nation as a whole. However, his absolute rule provoked unrest, and in 1934 he was assassinated by Croatian nationalists. His brother, Prince Paul, ruled on behalf of the young Peter II. In 1939, to calm Croatian unrest, Paul granted Croatia limited self-rule. But the future of Yugoslavia was now most threatened by the expansion of Nazi Germany under Adolf Hitler.

In 1945 the postwar fate of Yugoslavia was decided by the Allies.

In 1939 German troops invaded Poland. France and Great Britain declared war on Germany and Italy (the Axis powers), and World War II began. In 1941 Axis armies invaded Yugoslavia. The country was divided among Axis allies, and a puppet fascist Croatian state was set up to rule what was left, including Bosnia and Serbia. The Axis occupation was opposed by resistance groups, the Serbian Chetniks, and the communist Partisans. The Partisans, under the command of Tito, won support from Great Britain and its Allies, which now included the United States and the Soviet Union. In 1945, when the Axis powers were defeated, the Partisans took over power in Yugoslavia.

Josip Broz, known as "Tito," was born in Croatia in 1892. A metalworker by trade, he had become a local communist leader by 1927. During World War II, he led the communist Partisans against the Axis forces who were occupying Yugoslavia. They also fought the Croatian fascists and Serbian Chetniks. More than a million Yugoslavs were killed during the war, mostly by fellow Yugoslavs. In the early days of the resistance, the Chetniks, led by General Draza Mihailovic, were most successful. Their aim was to restore Serbian dominance in Yugoslavia, but Tito, winning support from Yugoslavs of all national groups, proved to be a better leader. In 1945 the Axis forces retreated before the armies of the Soviet Union. With the approval of the Allies, the Partisans formed a new government under Tito.

The Rise and Fall of Communist Yugoslavia

In 1945 the south Slav lands became a communist federation.

Tito's Yugoslavia was a popular place for Western tourists.

After World War II, Soviet forces occupied most of Eastern Europe. Communist governments were imposed or came to power. But Tito pursued an independent approach to economics and foreign policy. Yugoslavia developed its own brand of communism, unlike other nations in Eastern Europe.

In 1948 Yugoslavia was forced to separate from the union of communist countries because Tito refused to submit to Soviet orders. After 1945, there had been a growing rift between the Soviet Union and the United States, who was allied to the countries of Western Europe. When Tito split with the Soviets, Yugoslavia began to receive military and economic aid from the West. Cunning and ambitious, Tito remained a communist, but steered his country on a middle course between East and West. Throughout the 1960s and 1970s, he secured economic help from both the East and West to modernize Yugoslavia's industry and agriculture. Unlike other communist countries, Yugoslavia was open to visitors from the West. Tourism increased, further helping the economy.

Tito set up a federal Yugoslavia of six republics. Between 1945 and 1980, the republics were held together only by Tito's ruthlessness as a politician. He gave Croatia and Slovenia some local power that satisfied them temporarily. But when Tito died in May 1980, the new communist leadership faced great economic problems and found it very difficult to unite the republics.

Tension among the rival ethnic groups increased. Each of the republics elected a representative to act as president of Yugoslavia in turn, but in practice, Serbia was again the dominant force. The Slovenes and Croats believed that Serbia used its powerful position to redirect money and resources to Serb areas. They felt that they would do better as separate nations, with control over their own economies. As the 1980s progressed, there was growing unrest. In 1991 Slovenia declared its independence, followed by Croatia. Yugoslavia ceased to exist as a country.

Serbian leader **Slobodan Milosevic was central to the** collapse of Yugoslavia. He was born near Belgrade in Serbia in 1941. In 1989 he became president of Serbia. Milosevic came to power at a time of growing nationalist feeling among Serbs. In 1989 he annexed the province of Kosovo in southern Serbia, which had been semi-independent since 1945. The population there was mostly Albanian. When other republics argued for a looser federal structure, Milosevic insisted on a centralized system dominated by Serbia. When Slovenia and Croatia declared independence, Milosevic saw his chance to create a "greater Serbia" by annexing territories in republics with Serb minorities. War seemed inevitable.

In June 1991 celebrations followed Slovenia's independence.

Many Peoples, One Land

For 35 years, Tito managed to keep peace among the ethnic groups in Yugoslavia's republics. As the map shows, each republic contained a complex mixture of peoples. Many members of each group felt a greater loyalty to their people as a whole, settled throughout Yugoslavia, than to the federation.

ITALY

THE SERBS

The Serbian people predominated in Montenegro and in Serbia itself, but as the map shows, there were also large numbers of Serbs living in Bosnia and Croatia. Following the breakup of Yugoslavia in 1991, Serbs in these areas wanted to be united with Serbia itself. Because Serbia was once part of the Byzantine Empire, most Serbs belonged to the Orthodox Christian faith. In the province of Kosovo, in southern Serbia, the population was predominantly Albanian.

THE CROATS

With historic links to Hungary, most Croats were Roman Catholics. There were large numbers of Serbs living in some areas of Croatia. Croats themselves predominated in certain parts of Bosnia. Yugoslavia's two alphabets were another source of division within the country. Croats and Muslims used the Roman alphabet, which is also used to write English and French. Serbs used the Cyrillic alphabet, also used to write Russian.

THE BOSNIANS

Ruled by the Turks for 550 years, the Bosnian people were mainly Muslim, though some did not actively practice their religion. Large numbers of Croats and Serbs also lived in Bosnia. No other republic contained such a complex mixture of peoples. Although there were tensions, the different peoples of Bosnia coexisted peacefully. Muslim families enjoyed good relations with their Serb and Croat neighbors.

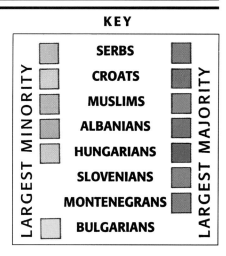

KEY

LARGEST MINORITY

LARGEST MAJORITY

SERBS
CROATS
MUSLIMS
ALBANIANS
HUNGARIANS
SLOVENIANS
MONTENEGRANS
BULGARIANS

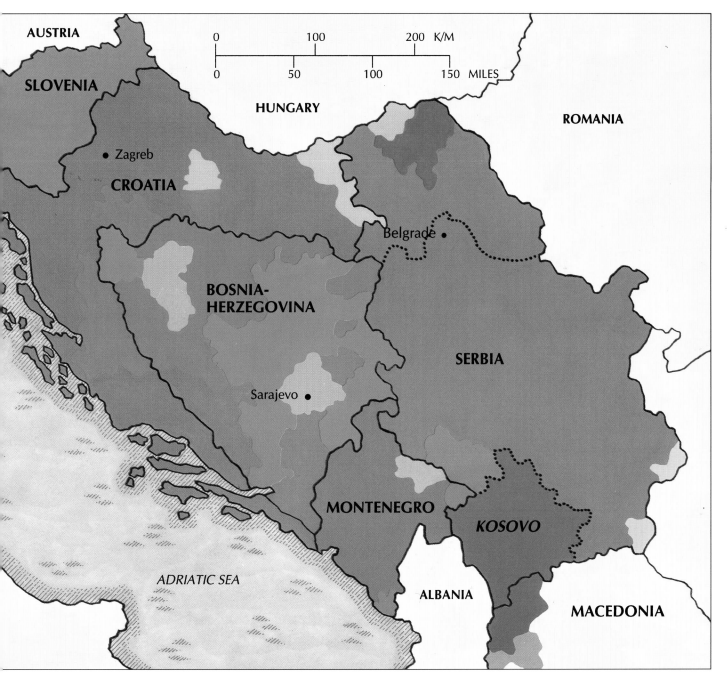

CAPT. M. STANLEY BRITISH/UN INTERPRETER:

"This is not a war as we understand it. The victims are not the combatants but chiefly the civilian population."

War Breaks Out in Yugoslavia

As Slovenia celebrated independence in 1991, Yugoslav air force planes flew overhead in a menacing show of strength.

Serb soldiers entered Vukovar in Croatia, in November 1991.

In the fall of 1991, the Yugoslav army withdrew from Slovenia. Leaving Slovenes in possession of their country, the federal tanks rolled into Croatia.

The Yugoslav army, controlled by Serbia, responded immediately to Slovenia's independence. Within days, federal troops invaded the republic. Fighting in Slovenia did not last long. Once Croatia, under its new president Franjo Tudjman, also declared independence, the Serbs concentrated on seizing territory there.

Croatian and Serbian forces

FRANJO TUDJMAN

Elected president of Croatia months before the republic declared independence. Some felt he used independence to gain power.

The Yugoslav army claimed to be intervening to protect Serb communities in Croatia. In fact, it wanted to seize as much of Croatia as possible and make it part of a greater Serbia. Serb rebels and Yugoslav troops bombarded the towns of Vukovar, Vinkovci, and Osijek in eastern Croatia, and the beautiful city of Dubrovnik on the Adriatic coast. Many civilians died. By the end of 1991, the eastern cities had fallen. Serbian forces occupied the region and declared it a new Serbian state, called Krajina.

The old walled city of Dubrovnik was shelled late in 1991.

fought in the fall of 1991.

Concerned by the bitter fighting, both the European Community and the United Nations tried to mediate a truce between Croatia and the Yugoslav government, now controlled by Serbia. But neither side would compromise. All over the world, people were shocked by reports of the Serbs' campaign of "ethnic cleansing" in Croatia. At the beginning of 1992, the United Nations sent large numbers of troops to Croatia to enforce a cease-fire, which left a third of Croatia in Serb hands. By spring, most of the fighting had died down there. But just over the border in Bosnia, it was about to begin.

The Conflict in Bosnia

In 1992 war in Yugoslavia spread to Bosnia.

In April 1992, Bosnia's claim to independence was recognized by the European Community. Serb forces immediately tried to seize power in Sarajevo. Between 50,000 and 100,000 people of all national groups protested, and the coup failed. But soon Bosnia was drawn into war.

Muslim leader Alija Izetbegovic is president of Bosnia. Since the war began, he has tried to prevent his country from being divided between Serbia and Croatia.

Radovan Karadzic is leader of the Bosnian Serbs. He wanted Serb forces to seize territory in Bosnia.

Serb tanks enter Bosanski Brod, a Bosnian town, in 1992.

In the spring of 1992, Serb militias and Yugoslav troops advanced on Bosnia's cities. They drove out hundreds of thousands of Muslims in a wave of "ethnic cleansing." The mainly Muslim Bosnian army was small and not well equipped, so they could not put up much resistance. However, some 15,000 armed Croats fought hard to protect their homes and, at first, cooperated with the Bosnian army.

Citizens of Sarajevo ran through the streets to avoid sniper fire.

In 1992 Serb forces advanced west and south from the Serbian border, capturing over 60 percent of Bosnia. The eastern towns of Srebrenica, Zepa, and Gorazde were attacked and bombed from the surrounding hills. The Bosnian army was forced to retreat. In western Bosnia, the Serbs also gained territory.

By 1993, Serbs held 70 percent of Bosnia. The Bosnian army was left in control of a narrow strip of central Bosnia that was sandwiched between two Serb-controlled areas. Sarajevo was in a separate area, surrounded by Serb forces, which also held the suburb of Grbavica. Trapped in the cities, inhabitants suffered as food became scarce and supplies of gas, water, and electricity were cut off. Many homes were destroyed by bombing and cannon fire attacks.

In early 1993, the Croatian army invaded the south of Bosnia in an attempt to steal territory. Ironically, this aggression was partly a response to a United Nations peace plan (see page 24) that had given Croatia control over the region. There, too, fighting was bloody. The United Nations voted economic sanctions against Yugoslavia and imposed an embargo, preventing the sale of arms to any of the republics. This meant that the Bosnian army became very short of weapons, especially heavy artillery. They did not have enough weapons to face the Bosnian Serbs, who were backed by Serbia and the Yugoslav army.

Serb forces mounted their attacks on Bosnia's capital, Sarajevo, from the hills above the city.

The Search for Peace

Around the world people were horrified by reports of the fighting in Bosnia. They were outraged by the senseless killing of civilians. Since 1992, the United Nations has been committed to an effort to bring peace to the troubled region.

In October 1992, British statesman, Lord Owen (above), and American diplomat, Cyrus Vance, produced a UN peace plan for Bosnia.

Yasushi Akashi is the UN secretary-general's personal envoy in Bosnia, conducting peace negotiations from the war zone itself.

UN secretary-general, Boutros Boutros-Ghali (center), escorted by UN troops

The 1992 Vance-Owen peace plan proposed to create ten self-ruling provinces within Bosnia, based on ethnic groupings. But in 1993 the proposal led to a new wave of fighting, as Croats tried to seize areas allotted to them in the proposal. By May 1993, it was clear that the plan had failed. During 1993 and 1994, talks continued. However, it has proved difficult to find common ground between the warring parties. President Izetbegovic wants Serbs to hand back some of the 70 percent of Bosnia they control. The Serbs insist on holding on to most of their gains.

Sarajevo Cease-fire Shattered

A peace conference on Bosnia in Geneva, Switzerland

The 1994 Sarajevo cease-fire was shattered after a "summer of hope." In September, the UN called in NATO warplanes to bomb a Serb tank that had violated the weapons exclusion zone around Sarajevo.

In October, UN soldiers found the mutilated bodies of 16 Bosnian Serb soldiers and four female nurses near Sarajevo. The deal for the reopening of Sarajevo was now threatened. By November, the fighting was increasing. When NATO combat aircraft were called in to warn off Bosnian Serbs and government forces, who had both violated the cease-fire, it put an end to the shelling. But soon afterward, two girls, a woman, and a boy were killed by sniper fire in Sarajevo. NATO sent warplanes to scare those who were responsible for these deaths. If incidents like these continue, Bosnia could again find itself at war.

Peace Hopes

In December Great Britain, France, Germany, Russia, and the United States tried to negotiate a new peace plan by offering Bosnian Serbs the prospect of political ties to Serbia. The allies insisted that this plan wouldn't be a step toward a "Greater Serbia," which is the Bosnians' worst fear.

General Rose (left) stepped down as commander of the UN forces on January 23, 1995.

Daily Life in the Cities

"The horror of dying like rats is not far from our thoughts."

In 1994 UN observers reported there were many people in central Bosnia near starvation because relief supplies were not getting through.

In this mountainous country, temperatures fall very low in the winter, and people are forced to scavenge for fuel in the snow. "I hope this winter does not last too long; I will have to burn the furniture to keep warm," stated one woman from Sarajevo.

Family and friends gather in Sarajevo to bury civilians killed by a Serbian explosive. Although many Bosnian churches, mosques, and other places of worship have been destroyed in the fighting, people still find places to pray. They pray for an end to the fighting, and for some solution that will bring lasting peace to their devastated country.

Only the metal beams remain of the bridge linking the two banks of the river in Sarajevo. Civilians must attempt to find their way across this dangerous structure.

Water remains in short supply in cities that are under siege. Long lines often form at wells, lakes, and streams. Civilians risk being hit by snipers' bullets as they struggle to haul buckets and water containers to their refuges, in cellars and burned-out buildings. Worse still, the water is often polluted. This adds the danger of disease to their many tragic problems.

A Devastated Country

It will take generations to heal the scars of war.

The damage created by years of war is extensive. In Sarajevo, planners estimate that over 60 percent of homes have been so badly damaged that they will have to be knocked down and completely rebuilt. It will take many years to repair the war damage that has taken place throughout Bosnia.

Bosnia is a mountainous country that has been cut by many steep valleys and deep gorges with fast-flowing streams. The mountains run parallel to the coast, which has always made east-west travel difficult. Transportation in Bosnia relied on a limited number of good roads and railroads. But together with factories and power plants, many of these have been destroyed. It will take years to rebuild the country's poor economy and damaged transportation networks.

The 16th-century bridge at Mostar was destroyed in 1993.

Evidence of acid rain

The Cost to the Environment

War has damaged the physical landscape of Bosnia, a country of great natural beauty. Bosnia contained many wilderness areas where wildlife was preserved. Forests have been destroyed in the fighting, and there is also evidence that acid rain has added to environmental problems. In the course of the war, sulphur dioxide and other gases have been released into the air. These gases mixed with water vapor in the air and fell as acid rain. The acid rain has affected the top parts of the trees, which died, and some forests have become lifeless. The habitats of birds, insects, and other animals have been destroyed, and the survival of many species is dangerously threatened.

"Life Will Never Be the Same"

Coming to terms with loss is very hard.

The fighting in Bosnia has changed most people's lives forever. Normal occupations, such as shopping and going to work or to school, seem a distant memory to most Bosnians.

In spring 1994 Sarajevo was quiet for the first time since the war began. The guns that had been surrounding the city fell silent and were withdrawn under UN supervision. The inhabitants now feel great relief, but grieve for the many who have died. Nothing has returned to normal. Streets are still blocked by the rubble of shelled houses and burned-out buses and trucks. Electricity has been slow to return. There is no work to speak of, no currency for buying and selling goods, and no way out of a city that is still surrounded by Serb forces. The same suffocating sense of being surrounded was experienced by Bosnians all over the country.

Historic Buildings Destroyed

Serb forces have systematically destroyed much of their enemies' culture and historic buildings. Mosques and minarets have not just been bombed, but in Bijeljina and Banja Luka they were blown up and burned to the ground. Shelling has destroyed the state and university library in Sarajevo and the Oriental Institute, which contained thousands of irreplaceable manuscripts on the Ottoman history of Bosnia.

A ruined Roman Catholic church in Sarajevo

Buildings blazed as shells rained down on Gorazde in the spring of 1994.

Can There Ever Be Peace?

The cease-fire achieved in Sarajevo in 1994 has not brought peace to the rest of Bosnia or the former Yugoslavia. Fighting continues around cities such as Tuzla and Gorazde, where, in the spring, 65,000 were trapped as Serb shells hit civilian targets.

The UN were powerless to stop the shelling of Gorazde, although the town had been declared a safe haven. One series of rockets hit the town's hospital, leaving ten dead and many wounded. The UN could only send in a few troops to report back on the fighting. Elsewhere the fighting has died down, and people are struggling to rebuild their lives. Nearly every family has lost fathers, mothers, aunts, uncles, and children in the conflict. Bosnians are asking themselves what they will do in the future, how they will pay for their food, and above all, when the war will finally be over throughout Bosnia.

Even during cease-fires snipers are active.

An Uncertain Future

As of the summer of 1994, it remained unclear whether Bosnia, Serbia, Croatia, and Slovenia could survive as independent countries. Would they be able to work together once the fighting is over? Another key question concerns Bosnia itself. It is uncertain whether Serbs will be allowed to keep the land they have

UN troops monitor Gorazde.

seized. President Izetbegovic is determined to negotiate Serb withdrawal from parts of Bosnia. But Serbs who have lost loved ones in the war vow never to surrender any territory. UN experts and local commanders doubt they will achieve a lasting peace settlement in Bosnia in the near future.

CHRONOLOGY

A.D. 1–99 Roman conquest of the Balkans

A.D. 400s Slavs arrived from central Europe.

1100s Bosnia emerged as a separate state under Kulin.

1328 Turks occupied Bosnia.

1389 Turks defeated Slavs at Kosovo.

1878 Austria-Hungary took Bosnia over from the Turks.

1914 Assassination of Archduke Franz Ferdinand

1914–1918 World War I

1918 Kingdom of the Serbs, Croats, and Slovenes was established.

1929 King Alexander declared personal rule over Yugoslavia.

1939–1945 World War II

1941 Axis powers invaded Yugoslavia.

1941–1945 Chetniks and Partisans opposed Axis forces.

1945 Yugoslavia was occupied by Soviet forces. Tito established a communist federation.

1948 Yugoslavia was forced out from the union of communist countries.

1980 Death of Tito

1980–1990 Rising ethnic tension in the republics

1991 Summer Slovenia and Croatia declared independence from Yugoslavia. The Yugoslav army, controlled by Serbia, entered Slovenia and then Croatia. Serbs began a campaign of ethnic cleansing.

1991 Fall A cease-fire in Croatia left a third of the country under Serb control.

1992 Spring UN peacekeeping force arrived in Croatia. Bosnia's independence was accepted by the European Community. Serb forces overran much of Bosnia and held cities, including Sarajevo, under siege.

1992 Fall Vance-Owen peace plan produced

1992 Winter UN troops were sent to protect the aid convoys.

1993 Spring Croats seized territory in Bosnia. Srebrenica was seized by Serbs. UN declared the cities of Tuzla, Zepa, Gorazde, Bihac, and Srebrenica "safe havens."

1993 Summer Heavy fighting in Mostar between Serbs and Croats. UN voted sanctions against Yugoslavia.

1994 Spring NATO air strikes forced Serbs to withdraw from Sarajevo and other cities.

1994 Summer Fighting continued around UN "safe havens."

Photo Credits
Special thanks to Frank Spooner Pictures, who supplied all the pictures in this book except
pages: 5 (top), 14, 15: Topham Picture Source; 10, 13: Hulton Deutsch; 11 (top): Bridgeman
Art Library; 12: Mary Evans Picture Library; 23 (top), 27 (both), 29 (top): Simon Townsley/Katz.

© Aladdin Books 1994, 28 Percy Street, London, W1P 0LD

Ο ΦΙΛΕΛΕ

ΗΜΕΡΗΣΙΑ ΕΦΗΜΕΡΙΣ

ΖΗΤΑ ΠΕΙΘΑ

erald INTERNATIONAL Tribun

PUBLISHED WITH THE NEW YORK TIMES AND THE WASHINGTON POST

London, Tuesday, March 8, 1994

immunity
ments that do not
plications for

immunity certificates
during his year at the
Home Office on security
grounds.

Clint
Is N

Des

Α ΚΑΙ ΘΑ ΣΥΓΚΑΛΕΣΕΙ

ΩN ΠΥ
ΕΥΡΩ

Σήμερα: Συνέρχον

Γαλανός: Συνάντη

Γράφει: Α.Λυκαύγης

ΤΙΣ σοβαρές του ανησυχίες,
εξελίξεις κι ενδεχόμενα
ρό-τ=ος της Δημοκρατίας Γλα
=ιμβούλιο την κατ
νέσθαι,

'Cleansers' of Muslims Show No Sign of Yielding

By Roger Cohen
New York Times Service

ZVORNIK, Bosnia-Herzegovina — Up through a ghostly terrain of smashed and ransacked former Muslim homes, Branko Grujic led the way, intent on showing off his crowning contribution to what he calls the victory of Serbian Orthodox Christianity over Islam in Bosnia.

Mr. Grujic, the mayor of this northeastern Bosnian town now controlled by Serbs and completely "cleansed" of its 40,000 prewar Muslim inhabitants, has a pet project. It stands atop the escarpment that overlooks Zvornik and the meandering sweep of the Drina River.

Arriving at the summit of the cliff, Mr. Grujic paused to kiss a wooden cross he has had erected before declaring. "The Turks destroyed the Serbian church that was here when they arrived in Zvornik in 1463. Now we are rebuilding the church and reclaiming this as Serbian land forever and

There is indeed a cruel finality to

of thousands of Muslims have been pushed out by force, many of them to Bosnian government-controlled territory around Srebrenica and Tuzla.

Such activity, and the uncompromising attitude of Mr. Grujic, suggest that Serbian readiness to accept new peace proposals from the United States may be scant.

Serbs in general remain committed to holding onto land they have seized by force and

The UN deploys troops around T
in preparation for an aid

appear to have little
Bosnian politic
with Mu

"Look
point
shif

KS

ure
ssue
ecurity

ell
rvice
ssions and blood-
h the Israeli-occu-
ael sent envoys to
Liberation
the first
ht the

موقف

تنبيله

واشنطن
رفيق خليل
من نيويورك
تونس
القاهر
الحد

د و
اسحق
مدينة
لبراهيمي
ضري
الضفة الغربية المحتلة)

فف بعد
(إبراهيمي
مصري

سجاد علي الحراش
على الحراش
سالت

Le gouvernement israélien divisé face aux colons extrémistes

tractations continuent en Israël à pro-
trée au gouvernement du parti
Tsomet du général Rafaël
hhaitée par M. Rabin,
gauche Meretz —
Shass, qui

opposé les membres du gouvernem
mesures à prendre contre les 25 000 et 30
veille, entre 25 000 et 30
dont quelques milliers
à Tel-Aviv pour réc
diate des extrém
occupés, voire, r
des colons.

EL

1 PRECIO: 100 PTS.

PIDEN «DEMOCRACIA PARIT

stras europe

Le Monde

75501 Paris Cedex 15

FONDATEUR : HUBERT BEUV

«...onstitución».

réndum será una prueba más de ...
Moldavia ha elegido un ...
la democracia, don-
...nos son

BOMB FEAR

53 DIE IN TR

ΙΤΙΚΗ ΗΓΕΣΙΑ

ΛΩΝ

ΤΗΣ

...is no cr...

...to be a very different thing...
...t suggested that the Republi-
...airly attacking him and added:
...n people will be outraged if any-
...is as an excuse for not doing the

DAILY MIRROR, Tuesday, March 8, 1994

CSA PAY BUNGLE
LEFT ME BRO

EXCLUSIVE
By ROGER TODD

ηνοί κομμάτων

Κληρίδη εκτάκτω

...οδήλως αρνητικές για την Κύπ...
...της Ευρώπης, συμμερίζετα...
...που: Σύντομα θα θέσει μπρο...
...ειμένου να δρομολογηθούν απ...
...αποτροπή χωριστής εκπροσώπ...
...σης των Τ/Κυπρίων.

Κι αυτό προκύπτει από χθε...
...νή συνάντηση του Προέδρο...
...με τον πρόεδρο της Βουλή...
...λέξη Γαλανό, που τον ενημ...
...νω σε κάποιες λεπτομέ...
...προαγονται στο...
...α το

A DIVORCED father
has wrongly had £634
a month docked from
his pay by the Child
Support Agency.

The outrageous bungle
has forced crane driver
Roy Sullivan to:
PUT his £40,000 house up
for sale.
SELL his Ford Escort
...ar, and
HAVE his phone cut off.
Desperate 36-year-old
...is now off work
...g from a stomach
...stress.
...the CSA
...puter for

agency fixed Roy's main-
tenance deductions at
£1,004 a month.
Then it found he was
being charged not only for
his two daughters – but for
a child who isn't his.
The agency apologised
and reduced the deduction
order attached to his
earnings.
But Roy, from Cardiff,
still hasn't had a refund.
He said: "I earn £300 a
week but after deductions
I didn't have enough left
to pay my £300 mortgage.
"I've had the 'For Sale'
...ign up for several weeks.
...erests of justice over-
...the PIIC does not
...my view."

My bank manager can't
see any option as I haven't
any money left to live on.
"I appealed against the
CSA assessment ...
summer but they ...
no notice. The ...
forced my emp...
hand it all over ...
"I can't bel...
dictatorial ...
agency behav...

Appa...

Labour ...
Jones, w...
Roy's ...
appalli...
Th...
bank...
big...
r...
l...

MUNDO

DEL SIGLO VEINTIUNO

...réis jamás; y si desesperáis seguid trabajando. (Burke)

...DIA INTERNACIONAL